SHARK
The Shredder

by Meish Goldish

Consultant: Melissa Carp
Aquarium Educator

BEARPORT
PUBLISHING

New York, New York

Credits

Cover, © Klaus Jost/Image Quest Marine and Farferros/Shutterstock; Title Page, © Klaus Jost/Image Quest Marine; 4, © Michael Patrick O'Neill/Alamy; 5T, © Splash News and Pictures/Newscom; 5B, © Splash News and Pictures/Newscom; 6L, © Splash News and Pictures/Newscom; 6R, © Splash News and Pictures/Newscom; 7, © Splash News and Pictures/Newscom; 8, © Douglas David Seifert/Oceans Image/NHPA/Photoshot; 9T, © Amanda Cotton/iStockphoto; 9B, © Mark Conlin/V&W/Image Quest Marine; 10, © Dorling Kindersley/Getty Images; 11, © David B Fleetham/Photolibrary; 12, © Jean Claude Carton/BCIUSA/Photoshot; 13, © Pacific Stock/SuperStock; 14, © Chris and Monique Fallows/Oxford Scientific/Photolibrary; 15, © Sigit Pamungkas/Reuters/Landov; 16, © Kelvin Aitken/age fotostock/SuperStock; 17T, © cbabbitt/iStockphoto; 17M, © Masa Ushioda/Alamy; 17B, © blickwinkel/Schmidbauer/Alamy; 18, © Tobey Curtis/FLMNH/NOAA; 19T, © Doug Perrine/SeaPics.com; 19B, © Andre Seale/ArteSub/Alamy; 20, © James D Watt/Stephen Frink Collection/Alamy; 21, © Pacific Stock/SuperStock; 22T, © Masa Ushioda/Visual&Written/BCIUSA/Photoshot; 22B, © Richard Herrmann/Oxford Scientific/Photolibrary; 24, © Rich Carey/Shutterstock.

Publisher: Kenn Goin
Senior Editor: Lisa Wiseman
Creative Director: Spencer Brinker
Photo Researcher: James O'Connor
Design: Dawn Beard Creative

Library of Congress Cataloging-in-Publication Data

Goldish, Meish.
  Shark : the shredder / by Meish Goldish.
    p. cm. — (Afraid of the water)
  Includes bibliographical references and index.
  ISBN-13: 978-1-59716-942-4 (lib. bdg.)
  ISBN-10: 1-59716-942-0 (lib. bdg.)
  1. Sharks—Juvenile literature. I. Title.

  QL638.9.G645 2010
  597.3—dc22

                              2009008724

For more information, write to Bearport Publishing Company, Inc., 101 Fifth Avenue, Suite 6R, New York, New York 10003. Printed in the United States of America.

10 9 8 7 6 5 4 3 2 1

Contents

A Sudden Attack

One night in 2007, college student Andrea Lynch and her friends hopped into a **dinghy**. They took it about 200 yards (183 m) from **shore** to another boat that was anchored in Sarasota Bay in Florida. They were looking for **bioluminescent** sea life.

Soon after reaching the boat, Andrea decided to go into the water to explore. As she floated on her back, Andrea suddenly started to scream. Something strong had sunk its teeth into her skin and was throwing her around. Andrea was being attacked by a shark!

Experts believe that Andrea was attacked by a bull shark similar to the one pictured here.

4

Andrea
Lynch

Andrea getting
onto the boat
before the attack

DANGER

Many sharks tend to be
most active at night.

Struggling to Survive

After the shark let go of her, Andrea swam back to the boat. Covered in blood, she told her friends what had happened. They knew that Andrea needed medical attention. However, during the attack, the dinghy had floated away. How would they get Andrea to a doctor? Luckily, someone had a cell phone and quickly called 911. In the meantime, Andrea's friends took off their shirts and pressed them against her **wounds** to stop the bleeding. Twenty minutes later, a rescue boat arrived and took her to a hospital. Andrea survived the attack, though she would never forget the shark's dangerously sharp teeth.

The shark's teeth marks on Andrea's back

DANGER

Andrea received 17 wounds on her back from the shark attack. Fortunately, no major **organs** were damaged. She needed more than 100 stitches to close up the wounds.

Andrea's healed wounds

Andrea's attack was the second one reported in 2007 in Sarasota County in Florida.

Three Big Biters

There are about 375 different shark **species**, though only about 12 are known to be dangerous to humans. Out of those 12, there are three types of sharks that bite people most often—bull sharks, tiger sharks, and great white sharks. All three are large, dangerous fish. The bull shark is about 11.5 feet (3.5 m) long, while the tiger is even longer at about 18 feet (5.5 m). The great white, the longest of the three, can grow to a length of about 21 feet (6.4 m).

The great white is the largest type of shark known to attack people.

The tiger shark gets its name because the young ones have stripes just like a tiger. Some lightly colored stripes can be seen on adults, too.

DANGER

About 50 to 75 people around the world are known to be bitten by sharks each year. Usually 10 to 20 of these victims die from their bites.

The bull shark gets its name because it rams its head into victims the way a bull does.

A Shark's Body

Though sharks differ in size, their bodies are alike in many other ways. For example, their skin is rough and scratchy, like sandpaper. They all have **gills** that allow them to get **oxygen** from the water so they can breathe. All sharks also have **fins** on their backs, sides, and tails, which help them control their movements while swimming.

Another way in which sharks are similar is that, unlike most fish, they have no bones. Instead, their skeletons are made up of **cartilage**. This rubbery material bends easily and allows sharks to twist and turn their bodies quickly in the water.

Unlike most other fish, there are no bones inside a shark's body.

A great white shark

fins

gill slits

DANGER

When sharks stop swimming,
they sink to the bottom of
the ocean. Their bodies lack
a swim bladder, a balloon-like
organ that most other fish
have to help them float.
However, their oily livers
and lightweight cartilage help
them stay afloat while they
are swimming.

11

Sharp Teeth

As Andrea Lynch painfully learned, many sharks have a dangerous bite due to their strong jaws and super-sharp teeth. Great whites, tigers, and bulls are among the types of sharks that have teeth with **serrated** edges—like the edges of a saw or a steak knife. Their jagged teeth **shred** flesh easily. They can even cut through bone.

Sharks do not chew their food. For small **prey**, they usually bite their victim once and then swallow it whole. For larger prey, they tear the meat into pieces and then swallow the pieces one at a time.

serrated edges

DANGER

Sharks have several rows of teeth, one behind the other. When a tooth is lost, another tooth from the row behind it moves in to replace it. It takes about a day for the new tooth to move into place.

Some sharks, such as this great white, grow and lose up to 20,000 teeth during their lives.

What's on the Menu?

Great white, tiger, and bull sharks use their razor-sharp teeth to catch sea animals to eat. They usually prefer animals that have lots of fat, since fat in their diet provides them with lots of energy. Some of their favorite prey includes bony fish, other sharks, and stingrays. Great white sharks also attack seals.

Sharks aren't interested in humans as food. However, they sometimes bite people that they mistake for sea animals. Other times they may bite swimmers who enter their **territory**. After biting a person once, sharks often lose interest and swim away, since humans don't have enough body fat to satisfy them.

Sharks, like this great white, have excellent senses to help them find food. They easily see, hear, and smell prey in the water. They also feel the water moving when animals are swimming nearby.

Sharks have few enemies. Their greatest enemies are people who hunt them.

DANGER

Tiger sharks eat almost anything they find in the ocean. They have been known to swallow glass bottles, metal cans, rolls of wire, leather boots—even steel oil drums! Tiger sharks are often called "swimming garbage cans."

Where Sharks Live

Sharks live in oceans around the world. Great white, tiger, and bull sharks can be found mostly in shallow water where people sometimes swim. While most sharks live only in the ocean, bull sharks can also be found in rivers and lakes that run into the sea.

Scientists are still doing research to learn about where and how far sharks travel. Many think that great white, tiger, and bull sharks migrate during the year. This means they move from one area to another. One reason for this could be that they are searching for food.

DANGER

Although great white, tiger, and bull sharks usually stay near the shore, they sometimes swim farther out into the ocean. Great whites have been found in water as deep as 3,215 feet (980 m)— many, many miles from shore.

Most sharks live alone, not in families.

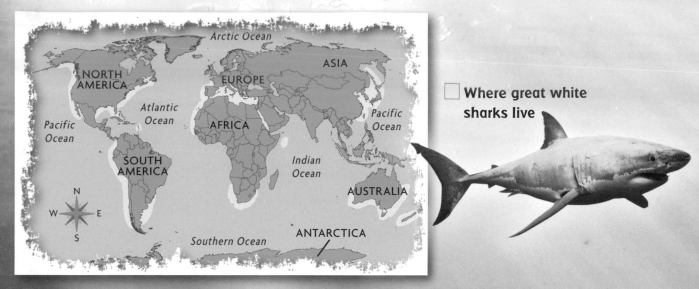

Where great white sharks live

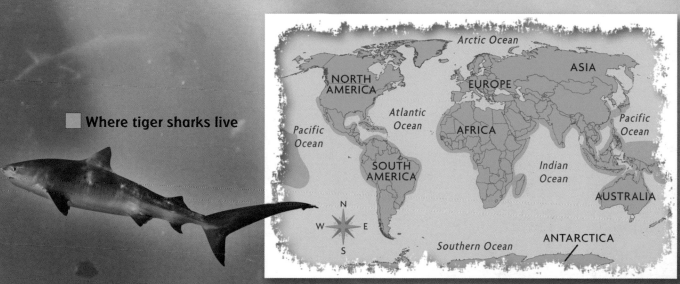

Where tiger sharks live

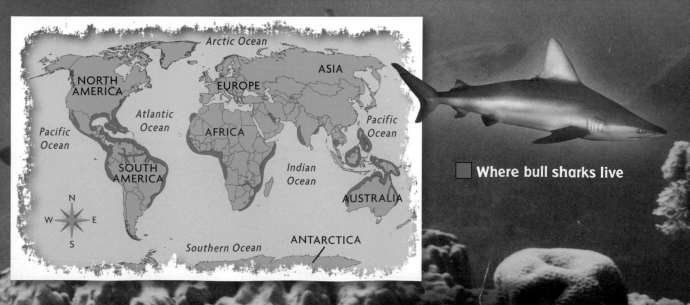

Where bull sharks live

Baby Sharks

All sharks give birth in the water, but not all of them give birth in the same way. Some kinds lay eggs that hatch outside the mother's body. However, sharks such as the great white, tiger, and bull give birth to live animals that grow inside the mother. Great whites and bulls usually have 2 to 12 **pups** at a time. Tiger sharks may have 10 to 80 pups at once.

Mother sharks don't take care of their young. Born with teeth, the pups are ready to hunt and shred prey on their own!

A bull shark pup

Some fish and other creatures eat young sharks, like these tiger sharks, so many do not survive. Those that do can usually live for about 20 to 30 years.

DANGER

Shark pups differ in size. Great white pups are about 4 feet (122 cm) long at birth, while baby bulls are about half that length at 2.5 feet (76 cm). Baby tigers are even smaller—only about 2 feet (61 cm) long.

In Case of a Bite

Few people will ever be attacked by a shark. However, those who are bitten can be in great danger. Experts offer this advice to bite victims.

1. Try to remain calm in the water.

2. If the shark tries to bite again, fight back. Hit the shark in its gills, eyes, or on the tip of its nose. The shark is likely to swim away.

3. Swim fast toward land but without splashing loudly. Sharks can feel and hear the water moving.

4. Once on land, wrap cloth around the wound to stop the bleeding.

5. Get medical attention immediately, no matter how small the bite is.

The best way to avoid shark bites is to swim only at beaches that have lifeguards. Also, always swim with a friend. Sharks are less likely to attack groups of people. If you do spot a shark—get out of the water immediately!

A great white shark

DANGER

People are more likely
to be killed by a car,
lightning, a bee sting,
or a snake bite than
by a shark attack.

Other Sharks with Dangerous Bites

Great white, tiger, and bull sharks are three kinds of sharks that are known to attack people. Here are two more sharks that also attack humans with their dangerous bites.

Oceanic Whitetips

- These sharks, which grow up to 13 feet (4 m) long, swim in the Atlantic and Pacific oceans. There are more oceanic whitetips than any other kind of shark.
- The oceanic whitetip has fang-like teeth with serrated edges.
- It circles its prey in order to catch it. The circle gets smaller and smaller until the shark finally attacks.
- Oceanic whitetips often eat turtles and birds as well as dead whales and dolphins.

Makos

- These dangerous sharks grow to 13 feet (4 m) long. They live in tropical waters around the world and generally swim near the shore.
- A mako shark has a pointed head and long, thin, sharp teeth. The teeth can be seen even when the shark's mouth is closed. Its teeth, however, are not serrated.
- Makos are among the fastest-swimming sharks in the world. They can reach a speed of about 40 miles per hour (64 kpm).

Glossary

bioluminescent (bye-oh-loo-*muh*-NES-ent) emitting light; living things that emit visible light

cartilage (KAR-tuh-lij) strong, rubbery material that makes up a shark's skeleton instead of bones

dinghy (DING-ee) a small open boat

fins (FINZ) flap-like parts of a fish that the animal uses to move and guide itself through water

gills (GILZ) the body parts of a fish that allow it to breathe underwater

organs (OR-guhns) parts of the body that perform a particular job

oxygen (OK-suh-juhn) an invisible gas found in water or air, which people and animals breathe

prey (PRAY) animals that are hunted by other animals for food

pups (PUPS) baby sharks

serrated (ser-AY-tid) having sharp, bumpy, or jagged points

shore (SHOR) the land along the edge of an ocean, river, or lake

shred (SHRED) to cut or tear

species (SPEE-sheez) groups that animals are divided into, according to similar characteristics; members of the same species can have offspring together

territory (TER-uh-*tor*-ee) an area that belongs to an animal

wounds (WOONDS) injuries in which the skin is cut

Index

Bibliography

MacQuitty, Miranda. *Shark.* New York: DK Publishing (2004).

Perrine, Doug. *Sharks.* Stillwater, MN: Voyageur Press (2002).

Simon, Seymour. *Sharks.* New York: HarperCollins (1995).

Read More

Arnosky, Jim. *All About Sharks.* New York: Scholastic (2003).

Gaines, Richard Marshall. *When Sharks Attack!* Berkeley Heights, NJ: Enslow (2006).

Pringle, Laurence. *Sharks! Strange and Wonderful.* Honesdale, PA: Boyds Mills Press (2001).

Schreiber, Anne. *Sharks!* Washington, D.C.: National Geographic Children's Books (2008).

Learn More Online

To learn more about sharks, visit
www.bearportpublishing.com/AfraidoftheWater

About the Author

Meish Goldish has written more than 200 books for children.
He lives in Brooklyn, New York.